AF477172

Extinctions

SHARMISTHA MOHANTY

Extinctions

cntxt

First published by Context, an imprint of Westland Books, a division of Nasadiya Technologies Private Limited, in 2022

No. 269/2B, First Floor, 'Irai Arul', Vimalraj Street, Nethaji Nagar, Allappakkam Main Road, Maduravoyal, Chennai 600095

Westland, the Westland logo, Context and the Context logo are the trademarks of Nasadiya Technologies Private Limited, or its affiliates.

Copyright © Sharmistha Mohanty, 2022

Sharmistha Mohanty asserts the moral right to be identified as the author of this work.

ISBN: 9789395073332

10 9 8 7 6 5 4 3 2 1

Typeset by Jojy Philip, New Delhi – 110015
Printed at Manipal Technologies Limited, Manipal

*For my parents and grandparents, long gone,
and an undivided Bengal, ancestral land*

Contents

Extinctions

Street

Long after the man with green coconuts has come to my door, holding out a
coconut with his right hand, his body and head just a little bowed towards
me as if this were a ritual, and perhaps it is, between him and me; after the
schoolchildren at the church school have all run out in a rush, flowing
over the steps and the slope and gone home, their mothers sometimes
waiting for them all day on the church steps; after the vegetable seller at
six and the fruit seller a few minutes later have parked their carts next
to each other so that it is easy for their customers and so they can share
stories in the lull when no one comes; after the gym has closed with its
slim women in tracksuits and Lycra so unsuited to this weather, and
the long imported cars parked in front of it have driven away; after the
trainers at the gym, Iqbal and Bernard, have finished their work and Iqbal
is perhaps doing his namaz on the wooden floor of the gym and Bernard
is packing his things; and Bernard told me the other day when I was there
that whatever you do here is fine, but really the best thing you can do is to
go walk by the sea at sunrise, what can be better than that; after all the thin
maidservants with protruding bones and a hurried walk have finished
their jobs of cooking and cleaning that will fill their whole lives till the
very end; after the tiny yellow birds have stopped flying in and out of the
tamarind tree, making the ripe tamarinds shake and fall; after darkening
shadows have taken away the old man who sits on his small balcony
staring out all day, near his staring face a huge palm leaf swaying like an
immense fan; after the sun has very, very slowly, moved down towards the
horizon and finally descended into the Arabian Sea in a vehement orange
glow and made it possible for the evening to begin, but only much after
the church bell rings for evening prayers at seven, and even after they are
over and people descend silently down the steps and the slope an hour
later, so that the day is lopsided; and an immense moon rises behind

the spire of the church; and in the plot next to the church four men sit
around a fire and make chapattis amidst the stacked bamboo, marble and
wood while nearby large rats wait for leftovers; and the chowkidars of
the buildings cook their dented vegetables for a solitary dinner without
their wives and children who are in the northern hills far away, so far that
it takes six days to get there memsahib, and as the dinner cooks they play
their wooden flutes, solitary notes and a few half formed melodies that the
evening sea wind takes down the street to the corner store where young
men smoke cigarettes; and the teenagers wearing spaghetti straps and
shorts and baseball caps lean against cars and move their bodies exactly
like the Americans they see on television; and eventually everything falls
silent, and not every window has a light; and the candles at the foot of
the statue of Mary at the bottom of the church steps and in the grotto on
the left are all burning still, which means it is a good day for someone
like me who likes to watch the flames but must depend on others to light
them; and the mango, tamarind, gulmohar and peepul trees can hardly
be distinguished from each other, although the moon has climbed higher
leaving the spire of the church alone against the dark sky; the shadows
of the palm fronds move slowly on the darkness of my wall, and the
clouds slowly, slowly, over the sky; now the street takes a long breath and
the candle flames on the church steps begin to tremble and the steps
themselves; the trees lean close towards each other to form a forest, so
that I could be wandering in its vastness away from the world, searching,
searching for what ought to be my life but is not; emerge again, onto the
street's dark spine, wondering whether I wait to live or if waiting is also
living; the street never forces a choice; it allows the alternation of insight
and emptiness; when insight sharpens and has nowhere to go it turns
into emptiness which slowly gathers strength to become insight again;
now the street exhales, stirring the fallen leaves that choke the gutters, but
keeping to itself the uncontrollable fluctuations beneath things, revealing
only flames from Diwali and stars from Christmas, old couples who have

                    SHARMISTHA MOHANTY

settled a lifetime of differences and now walk together in great peace, the church bell which is loud enough to wake us at dawn if we are already aware of the half light, and soft enough not to if we are sleeping, and as the street exhales and sways, the darkness above comes closer, closer, and there appear a few incisive stars that have cut open the sky of smog and dust and smoke.

Spring

The body can be gathered and bent forward at a slight tilt, offering a glass of water to quench the thirst of someone it respects. At times, only the head and shoulders may bend downward, hand on the heart, to thank someone for that which lies a great distance beyond language. The street, has received both of these gestures. But this is a different time. The slender, elongated light of winter disappears, suddenly. The light turns muscular, overcomes earlier restrictions. The koel arrives, heralding so much more than spring, stirring hopes that can be realised only through the most untiring grit and determination.

The body turns inside out now, and the most noxious things are set free. They rise into the air, not from the desire for flight but through the force of despair. The air is thick with bird and song. Spring has brought birds from wherever they have been all year, and the memory of hill and plain and forest in their call expands the space the street occupies. When the body tears, some things spill and split like vicious seeds. Others, which already have their own stunted life, drag themselves over the asphalt, cripples whose legs end at the stumps of knees, holding a broken stone wall for support, hunchbacks who will never see the sky above.

They crawl and drag themselves past the seller of berries and raw mangoes who no longer stands in the light and has moved to the shade, on the opposite side of the street. His wooden cart is an ancient discovery but when he raises his left arm and runs a hand through his hair, a watch gleams in the light. His knowledge of time is not as ancient as his need. It is the one who stands watching whose knowledge of time is old, almost geological. Children eat the berries sprinkled with black salt, tart and pungent on the tongue. Those things in the body that have not emerged onto the street are still inside, things smashed many times and held together by spittle, uncertain glue. Evening will come later now, after the schoolchildren have eaten their berries and gone home, but it will come. The falling light will cover over narratives turned the wrong way around, of desire after fulfilment, of the closure of what has not even begun. It will bring the knowledge that every life turns, somewhat like the universe, but coming into the light only according to its own season.

The birds do not return to their trees. They skim the flames that someone has already lit in the grotto without ever burning their wings. Inside the house a luminous soul fights the darkening patina of need. There is utter silence as this need searches for a new moral sense with which to look at itself. The search will begin here, but go far afield, through people and places in other continents.

A tree falls and breaks the top of a stone wall. The sound is an explosion whose echoes go deep into the corners of the rooms, into dishes and bookshelves. The fishtail palm has broken exactly at one of the chalk-white rings on its tall trunk which marked its destiny. It flowered from the top, the flowers small green balls, hanging together in enormous bunches. Only one level flowered at a time, over the years. After twenty years perhaps, the lowest level flowered, and that meant the tree was nearing its end. The trunk will be cut in two for channelling water, the fibres will be used for fishing lines, and the base made into a huge bucket for lifting water from river or well.

The street is like a flame in a windless place.

Call

At first, the call. Only later its precise meaning. The seller is always solitary as he walks and calls, and it is only this solitude which joins the seller to his opposite, the one who sits in a room by a window, confronted not by the heat or an accusing customer but by his own shadowed life. What they sell is made from the soil, the sea, the human hand.

A devastated ocean surrounds the city, lined with excrement, trash and shreds of coloured plastic bags hanging from the branches of its coastal mangroves, somehow still bringing waves to a shore of black rocks and offering a real horizon. From a fragile fishing boat on this ocean, the curves of the coastline assume a map's precision, the angle at which the coconut trees lean left indicates the direction of a recurrent wind, and at a distance the land assumes a great silence, an essential silence of the earth, composed of the sounds of eternal things.

They bargain with slyness, anger, humour, abandon, tenacity, sadness, but they are always endowed with a human dignity whose source will remain forever unknown. And the visitors who come from lands where confidence grows wild watch the street but in the end find no beauty where want exists, they are so sure of universal values, so sure of the universe.

Reed mats, bamboo flutes and mangoes make the street immense. It is not only from where mangoes, reed mats and bamboo flutes come, but from when, and the street travels through the history of the world. The history of the world, the street fears, is not layer upon layer, but sequential, where things simply replace one another. Now, the ones who come most frequently are those with long, battered iron carts who take away broken and useless things.

In the fading light there remains only a melon's luminous curve.

As evening comes, the fruit seller arranges carefully the fruits that housewives have endlessly looked through to get the best, get their money's worth, and he calls out his last calls, waits again for women to come and undo what he has just arranged, and after that happens a few times over and he finally leaves, still calling, it is as slowly as he came, pushing the weight of the cart, the iron wheels turning slowly in the darkness.

In every seller an original patience lives in the soles of the feet, in the pelvis and the spine, and in the hands that weigh and measure and count, a physical patience they cannot refuse, a kind of knowledge that can never be lost, but which can break suddenly once and for all.

The call can bring its listener back to life.

Threadbare

When a great loneliness has been attained, when there is no assurance, when the self is threadbare, ragged at the edges, when a life is so shaken out and empty that there is room in it for every object and being it watches, it is then that the ragged self sees through the muscular light, through the complex, melodic call of the unknown bird which never shows itself, and does not stop seeing, it finds a transparency in things that leads to their sources, whether that be a season or a man, the black clay horse with a benign sadness in its eyes leading to the hands of its maker, so nothing seems to have a definite end, and it moves towards each thing as easily as night towards day, so that the distinction between what is human and what is not falls away, and this is a knowing that cannot be lost as strength can or the ability to love, from this an unbreakable power unleashes itself that looks from the outside like complete powerlessness, and the evening wind from over the sea makes that threadbare self billow like a tattered sail, all that resisted it now become the air on which it rises, so that what has come to stay, can regard the clear spring night, regard the new stars, regard the different trees, as variations on a life span, each not to itself but to the other standing witness.

The Horse

In the village unsold horses stand by the dozens in dark, small rooms. The hand that dusts them sometimes and lets in the sunlight also lets the dust fall on the ground. It would be too much work to remove all the horses and sweep the floor and put them back again. The dust swept off the horses falls below and grows in thickness, piles up over the months and years, till the horses stand up to their chests in a forest of dust.

Above the closed rooms, the International Space Station moves swiftly across the dark night sky, the brightest and swiftest thing in the darkness after the moon. It appears 10 degrees above North-North-West and disappears 10 degrees above South-East.

On the red soil plains of Bankura centuries ago, no one knows quite how, the fired clay horse became an offering to the gods. It was given in gratitude when a child began to crawl, offered so a wish could be fulfilled. It was found on the tombs of saints. The cow, the bull and the elephant lived beside all that was everyday. The horse was never everyday, never a fact, and the maker of the fired clay horse may never have seen one with his own eyes.

The horse is not native to these plains, or even to the subcontinent. It came from somewhere too far to walk, from as far away as the most unreasonable desire, the most devastating hope.

The horse came from Central Asia, very likely before the Aryans, but certainly with them over the mountains, as they moved into the subcontinent. Then centuries later again with the Mughals, and once more with the British, this time in ships over the sea. Many died from seasickness.

Thirty-one fired clay horses, almost three feet high, stand at the bottom of a banyan tree, an offering to the gods. They have wide jaws, long necks, stout legs, saddles carved with flowers and leaves, and small tails.

Leaving behind the red soil of Bankura, the horse enters living rooms, with its solemn, vigilant face, an object separated from its use, matter lasting so much longer than human gesture.

On the International Space Station an orange zinnia flower blooms.

In the fierce heat of May once, on this red soil parched with thirst, we looked deep into a well, into dark water which healed our scorched eyes, we saw ourselves reflected among yellow and brown fungus floating on the surface. Someone lowered a tin mug into it and scooped up the water, and we drank and drank, we quenched our thirst, and instead of being ill from the fungus and moulds we were well as never before, and when night came, we could see again, so we lay down on the red earth and looked up at a new sky of stars.

The horse was a wish for the power of the conquerors, even more it was a wish for boundless spaces, a wish for the inexpressibly wide and broad, for the whole earth as well as the skies, for the unharnessing of human life.

Every day, as it circles the earth, the International Space Station sees thirty-two nights and dawns.

Sunset

Every day something else sets over the subcontinent along with the sun. Today it is the crouched man, sullen and taciturn. Hundreds of horses have sprung from his hands. There is mud on his feet, mud on his fingers, his skin is withered from working with water and earth. Crouched, he travels towards his own extinction. He wants to whip the future which is always somewhere else, wants to watch it whimper in terror, wants to shatter its complacent stride forever. Only the trees and rivers have a future that stays with them, wherever they are. He is jealous of the sun which will rise again. He crouches and turns his face away from the light, turning and turning away till his neck can swivel no further. His sons do not crouch near the potter's wheel, with erect spines they leave to work as sweepers in humid, dilapidated, malarial government offices. The horses he made never looked him in the eye. Their gaze was always turned towards infinity. That same infinity that cares nothing for the movement of time, does not acknowledge the future, that crucible of fate. That same infinity that spills endlessly from the eyes of god. No moon and stars follow in the darkness that comes after the crouching man sets. Like other things become extinct, he rotates on his own axis. If he looked up he would see palm-leaf fans revolve, and scalloped bell metal bowls, and clay pitchers, each thing made by the hand, related like planets.

The Emperor Jehangir, with his hand on the flank of an Abyssinian zebra, revolves in that same darkness. The zebra was given to him as a gift in his sixteenth regnal year, 1621. Jehangir repeatedly touched the animal to see whether the stripes on it were painted. He had never ever seen anything like it before. 'One might say that the painter of fate, with a strange brush, had left it on the page of the world,' he wrote. Zebras still run in the plains and grasslands of Africa, Jehangir is conserved in his portraits and monuments, it is the awe that is extinct, part of a species of emotions in which the centre is outside the self.

Ustad Mansur, master painter at the Emperor's court, painted the zebra at the Emperor's orders. The zebra looks towards the right, held close within a border decorated with flowers and leaves.

History

He has a face built by everything the earth has thrown up and the sky sent down. He sits in his thatch-roofed hut and watches. His mouth is open, his teeth are rotting. He sits on the edge of the hut, on the edge of the ravine. In the ravine, no river, no stream, nothing moving. The fish that rest on the bottom are carved from dark silver, inedible.

Following the ridge of regrets, fate, thoughts that came too late, a future appears, even of the past. Untamed, animate, time becomes many, and landscapes continue to be formed, not naming themselves yet, not conscious of being an island or a continent.

On the blackened iron scales in the marketplace, a thousand years equals today.

We Are

We are the slow churning of cement mixers, the leaden mass of concrete, we are the pools of fresh water at construction sites from where the Aedes mosquitoes rise with the sun, we are the debris of old mansions grown useless, the grey air filled with enormous particles of dust hanging low in the early morning light, we are the strained breath and the respiratory infection, the pneumatic drill that bores through our visions, we are our deflated pasts no matter where they were, inflated futures always in the future, the fevered, dengue-ridden present, the stench of urine from roadsides and bushes and vacant plots is our own stench, making an ornament out of sudden flowers, we are the flared temper which lights our way, the leper begging with his stumps since the hands that move and create life are long gone, we are the holes in the road through which we fall but never far enough, we are the rising prices and the broken buyers both, the lit candles, the flowers offered, the bruised knees and hands of prayer, the din of rituals, the used up rag of belief, we are the women in crowded banks that lock in the smell of sweat, planning their savings so they can leave—for New Zealand, Australia, Canada, America, Dubai, Hong Kong, Singapore, we are the streetlights dimmed by the hazy night, and all that cannot be tamed is far away, a lake by a hill, a river's looping course, we are the lonely skywalks at night where idle men wait to attack exhausted women going home, we are falling debris, dust and mud, we are rising steel and iron and glass, an Alpha city like Milan, Madrid and Moscow, impacting the whole world, falling against it, pushing it on its axis, we are the man slamming a woman's head against the windshield of a sedan as he drives, we are the man who is passing by that calls the police, we are the police who ask him to call a different police station, under a heinous sky the irascible wind blows, we are the roads whose innards are dug up and heaped on either side, we are the stumps of trees chopped down to make

room for these roads, trees that have been hacked by ebony coloured men
as if they were hacking at the body of god, the same men whose ancestors
would have broken stone to build god's body and his home, we are the
traffic permanently stalled where patience and impatience must alternate
like inspiration and expiration and the ambulance that has right of way
is deeply resented, we are the young men who break the nose of someone
who tells us not to litter as the sun sets over the sea next to us, we are the
miniscule artificial gardens where only the very old hobble forward, the
cratered pavement with a jutting brick or an iron rod sprouting forth that
will trip us up, we carry the heat on our backs like a sack of stones, only one
day in winter is there a benevolent light blue sky, and sleep when it comes
is held at bay by regrets that rise like reflux in the throat, or shredded by
packs of stray dogs that bite the darkness, we are the ocean wrecked by the
garbage in our gut, moving slowly with a long way to go, because only very
far away, thousands of miles from here, will we become pure, with only salt
and fish and weeds and the wind.

Kajol

Bring the bell metal lamp stand and set its bell metal prodip on top. Pour in the ghee, place a wick in it and light the flame. Let it catch and for a few minutes, watch it burn, watch it bend. Appease the longing for a living light. When the middle-aged housemaid, widowed as a young girl, watched the flame, she watched it with attention, dreaming of marriage perhaps, of things that would never come again. Then bring the kajol lata, open it, line it with a little ghee, and hold it close to the flame. It is a brass container shaped like the body of a small fish, with a tail at the end, where it slides open, revealing its two identical parts, concave inside like a shallow bowl. A grandmother, after a lifetime of steadiness, would have held it perfectly straight, one side over the flame, the other away. Her dreams were already fulfilled and she would think, as she watched the flame, about the spices to be ground that evening or the fish to be cooked. But then as she kept watching her mind would go away from the daily work, to the stars she had gazed at the night before as she sat on the terrace by herself at the end of the day. *The earth, in a certain way, meditates.* As the flame burns the soot rises to the inside of the kajol lata, and deposits there in layer after layer. Light creates its opposite—a deep darkness. On the International Space Station a flame is not long and flickering, it is blue and spherical and steady, without smoke. *The atmosphere, in a certain way, meditates.* The grandmother would line her infant granddaughter's eyes with the new kajol. For the infant child, that wrinkled forefinger and its roughness at the edge of the eye would mean the touch of unequivocal love, forever. Holding the kajol lata over the flame for two hours, the arm will have to change its position many times. Looked at long enough, the time it takes to make enough kajol, the flame takes away the past and the future. After the deepest black kajol is made, thick inside its container, add a little ghee once again to make it moist and smooth. A mother incapable of dreaming used her forefinger to line her own eyes and this brought out her disconsolate beauty. A minute amount of water rose in her eyes as a response to the kajol, for just a moment, and then subsided.

Gesture

This is the gesture the grandmother used the most, with her rough palm, crooked fingers and hardened, uneven nails. She held the chin of another lightly, with her right palm. The one handed gesture happens between the older and the younger and more often between women. It is less definite than holding a face in both hands, or gathering another in one's own arms, more precarious. The face is held at the point where it spreads the least yet where its completion is acknowledged. The receiver will usually smile, expanding the muscles at exactly the places where the other's palm rests. And the giver will usually tilt her head a little to the left, in the direction opposite to her holding palm. They will both look at each other. Not an embrace, not a kiss, but a more asymmetrical affection, a gesture the maid could make towards the little girl she looked after every day.

If each person's place in the world was fixed so were the sources of their joys and sufferings. Now we move with ease, and our sufferings leap upon us, feral and devastating.

Abhimaan

In Sanskrit, abhimaan is arrogance, pride. The word is definite and closed. Great classical languages have words for the grand emotions, the most complex philosophical insights. When this word comes into Bengali, it loses its rigidity, it gathers moisture, firm earth giving way to a sudden, still pond into which trees gaze, so numerous in the Bengal landscape. It changes in meaning to a sense of self which has been wounded, and which cannot have, or does not want to have, any direct expression of that wound. This can occur only between those who share the most vulnerable of relationships—lovers, parents and children, the nearest of friends. Bengalis are a loquacious people, but in abhimaan, there is silence. It is on the face, in a gesture, in the eyes, and if there are tears they are held at the edge and rarely overflow. In a woman the drape of the sari could almost hide it. We are an argumentative people, but in abhimaan there is no argument or fight. The pond is silent but aware, whether at noon, when the trees protect it from the harsh light, or at night, when some distant nightglow makes it luminous. The word combines the tender and the tough, in a way that the two sometimes lose their separateness. It belongs with other emotions like respect, or surrender, that are disappearing because the self now refuses to bend. Abhimaan assumes a childness, a kind of wound and love, or wounded love, of which only a vernacular is capable, a daily tenderness, a contiguous self, a searing need for the other. Tigers still wander in the mangrove forests of Bengal. There are words that give expression to the inclination of a culture. The long sound of abhimaan indicates a feeling that doesn't simply come and go, but stays, for hours, days, months. This expression reveals something of the Bengali soul, its exaggerated sense of self come together with its genuine capacity for feeling.

Kantha

My father's sister is making a kantha for me. The old silk sari she uses is white, with a black border and tiny black flowers at intervals on the white ground. The kantha is made of layers of this soft silk and my aunt holds all the pieces together with a light green thread, luminous against the black and white. She lives downstairs and when she comes up to sit with us, she often brings the kantha and works as she talks. A kantha was always made for someone else, a niece, a sister, a child. Over that month she was making it, her love for me, the only child of her one brother, spoke every day. Otherwise, the love was always there, holding deep and steady. But through this cloth and the green thread, it was being brought into the light. As her fingers threaded the needle, tossed the cloth and placed it on her lap, matter and action came together to make her love more manifest. It was in the making that her love spoke the most, more than when the kantha was finished. The process was akin to loving, which is always in movement and without destination.

Stairs

From the main door, past the old hatstand with its shining mirror, the stairs went all the way to the upper floor. A grandfather in his dhoti went up slowly when he came home from his walk. The stairs were grey cement with a tall window at the landing halfway where the light came in. A daughter ran down joy to meet her father. A father climbed pain. Servants walked up exhaustion. A wife climbed what should be. These stairs allowed the body time for anticipation to grow, to conceal disappointment, to prepare for sharp encounters, to slow down after an unexpected defeat. The stairs were neither inside nor outside, a place where the world had been left behind or not yet begun. A daughter climbed up devastation in her snow boots from another country, slow and heavy. A father was brought down as a dead body, covered with flowers. The men in the family carried the stretcher and maneouvered it at the halfway landing so they could turn at the right angle. The banister had been grasped a thousand times. It was down these stairs that people in the family came when they were leaving, for distant worlds, for the stars, travelling through the darkness of the universe. It was up these stairs that they came when they returned, to a home transformed by their own being away, the grandparents waiting for them on the final step, as if unchanged, with their natural calm, the sunlight behind them.

Paper Stars

With the grime in our lungs and the soot in our throats we can no longer speak, our roads are shattered we can no longer walk, there are grills on our windows we can no longer fly, our skin is covered with rashes from mites in our beds so we can no longer feel, with the grit in our eyes we can no longer see, our eyelids have tiny black growths on the inside, allergic responses to the angry air, when we look we can no longer distinguish one thing from another, at dawn the smog hangs low and ominous but we manage to reach evening, the only stars that hang above the alleyways are dim paper stars made in China, but we care nothing for origins and though we know that what is ruined is better for the soul than what shines, our instincts are ground down by doubt, like our ancestors wanted, we have nothing left but our consciousness, fluttering like the inexorable wings of pigeons and crows who feed on our leftovers.

Prayer

This is the prayer of the swaying ladder and the broken wooden stool that
lean against a wall where grime runs down like rain, this is the prayer of the
alleyways, of punctured cement bags, dented buckets, clothes washed too
many times hung out to dry, of rusted iron pipes, caved in paver blocks, the
alcoholic stooping low on his plastic chair in the middle of the alley, things
made unsteady by endurance and fortitude, and nothing here is whole
except a pair of crutches standing gleaming against a boarded window,
above all of this hang lit paper stars across the narrow space between the
walls, at the deep end of an alley an icon in a glass case is lit in red, once
again this is the season for lights and stars, *give us the new, the unbroken,* the
street that the alleys open onto has seen the world pass from the age of
coal to the age of oil, and its carved wooden balconies hang above, broken
and tilted, in these houses generations live their lives, the street winds and
curves, and in the ruins of the largest house a thorny bush fills the main
doorway over which golden lights glow, there is no room to hide here on
the narrow street, in the alleys, and all that is brutal stands revealed, there
are stars over the moss and plants that have risen from the dark crevices
in the alley stone, the crippled man trembles and shakes as he takes half
an hour to walk from one end of the alley to another, *give us the new, the
unbroken,* little children jump off piles of cement bags, and because nothing
shines here except the stars and the lights they speak the prayer that words
cannot, shining over the air, over the alleys and battered roofs, over each
thing as precarious as prayer, and through the evenings the lights slowly
reveal the poise of the street and the alleyways, the poise of the swaying
ladder and the broken stool, *give us a change more muscular than the seasons,*
the unrepaired bicycle with one wheel gleaming in the paper starlight.

City

Underneath the asphalt and newly laid paver blocks the city is pulled forward and sideways with the arms of soil excavators, it revolves with the lugubrious exertion of cement mixers, rises with hesitating deliberation in cranes, quivers on the flyovers, is crushed down under its own dumps, each motion against the body's rhythm, so that feet are always in search of balance. The old man in white who sits at the corner where four arterial roads meet, under the rise of a flyover, in his attar shop raised well above the ground, is one of the few who holds steady. He pours attar from an enormous glass bottle into a tiny one the size of a thimble, and he doesn't spill a single drop.

After he tightens the stoppers on both bottles he begins to speak of mountain herbs from which these attars are made, of mountain roots, and of abandoned mountain lakes. The buyer suddenly wonders whether this city is an immense human error. Then the mind tells itself not to compare or see the mountains as a more correct landscape. Here, even the most instinctive longing doubts itself. As he turns towards the street, he sees the flyover where the May sun is burning the metal roofs of a hundred cars in the stalled traffic all the way till the horizon. There, the sky is a venomous blue cut by cranes at the height of towering buildings under construction, he counts and there are eleven, and the abandoned lake returns. The old man begins his namaz on the white sheet that covers the floor of his shop.

The city is balanced, dangerously, on the axes of religious faith and construction, both turned, always, towards the future.

Mourning

A tapir moves on the banks of the Las Piedras river in the Amazon forest. Behind him, the banks rise into low, green cliffs dense with vegetation and trees. The tapir moves very slowly, looking down at the ground, prehistoric animal walking with the weight of the millions of years that his species has been here, with each step moving from his origins till today.

Mourn the sight dimmed from sewing up the near, the lost measure of the near and the far, mourn the indivisible individual, the assertions that lash the air, mourn the end of what can be attained only by asking, the time when deep was the depth, mourn the fatal arrhythmia at the heart of things, the faltering of wings and eyelids and hands and breath.

Smile

It has taken thousands of years to attain this smile, the moving from what is to what can be. The body implicated in touch and force, extension and motion. The face quiet, the lips closed. On the face a smile, not of delight or satisfaction, but a smile almost imperceptible, the minutest movement of the closed lips. Always on the faces of the gods, but also the apsaras on temple walls, the dvarpalas, the sculpted couples sitting in love, the courtesans, the monks.

Almost imperceptible this smile, but leaving itself behind even on stone faces that are smashed, on broken lips and eyelids.

The eyes that had to look far and discern danger, the predator in the high grass, the enemy behind the hills, could perhaps turn inward after centuries had passed. It has taken thousands of years to learn this smile, for us to know that it is not just for the gods. Never a face that suffers, in stone or wood or clay. Always the face composed and poised, equivalent, not denying suffering but including it.

In a desolate museum near a small, medieval town, a solitary caretaker sits on a broken wooden chair. Among the weeds and tall grass behind him are faces and bodies made of stone, standing under the open sky, the smile worn down by sun and rain and dust. Some lie on their sides on the soil. Dusk falls here with the weight of a thousand years. The caretaker has been here since he was a young man and he has now, after decades, understood the smile.

How it rises, from the spine upwards, with the body's sap and blood and breath—unbreakable.

Facts

Forty tons of cosmic dust fall on the earth every day, collecting on the roofs of buildings and sidewalks and park benches, each particle barely the width of a human hair. In Kerala god can be a mirror, Kannadi Bimbam, a reflection of the self rather than a deity. The German poet Georg Trakl was supported by Ludwig Wittgenstein through a time of hardship. When he read Trakl's poems he said, 'I don't understand them. But their *tone* makes me happy. It is the tone of true men of genius.' The Rig Veda says that among the things that fly the mind is the swiftest. In 1590, Abul Fazl, the court historian of Emperor Akbar, wrote, 'The written letter looks black, notwithstanding the thousand rays within; or it is a light with a mole on it that wards off the evil eye. A letter is the portrait painter of wisdom; a rough sketch from the realm of ideas; a dark night ushering in day; a black cloud pregnant with knowledge; the wand for the treasures of insight; speaking, though dumb; stationary and yet travelling; stretched on the sheet yet soaring upwards.' In the village of Pathra in Bengal, on the banks of the Kangsabati river, a devout Muslim man has spent his life repairing and restoring medieval terracotta temples near his home. From the entire Vedic age, 1500 BC to 500 AD there remains not a single piece of concrete material—not a monument or a jewel, a coin or a weapon or a bowl. What remain are words—hymns, ritual instructions, philosophical explorations. The pioneering Bengali scientist Jagdish Bose worked for many years to show that plants have life and respond to light, heat, trauma, shock and toxins, exactly as humans beings do. He said, 'It was when I came upon this mute witness of life and saw an all-pervading unity that binds together all things—it was then that for the first time I understood the message proclaimed on the banks of the Ganga thirty centuries ago—*They who behold the One, in all the changing manifoldness of the universe, unto them belongs eternal truth, unto none else, unto none else.*' In the subcontinent, since the beginning of agriculture, there has been an abundance of food crops. Staples of rice, wheat, millets, seeds from which oils could be pressed, a profusion of vegetables and fruits, spices for taste, milk, butter, curd. There was no need to take life. Scholars say the idea of ahimsa arose perhaps from this simple fact. 'And while I stood there I saw more than I can tell and I understood more than I saw, for I was seeing in a sacred manner the shapes of all things in the spirit, and the shape of all shapes as they must live together like one being,' said Black Elk of the Oglala Sioux people, describing a vision he had as a child.

Rta

The word '*rta*' occurs 450 times in the 1,008 hymns of the Rig Veda.

It has no exact counterpart in a modern language.

It is a kinetic word, a meaning field, expansive.

Rta is the wide and free space where the cosmos has its being, where all things in the universe can dwell. The dawn begins its journey from the dwelling of *rta*, and moves along the path of *rta*, as do the visions of the seers. The sun is its shining face. It is the safe path along which both light and men may travel. It is the innate attribute of things by which they are what they are. The *rta* of water is to seek a lower ground. It is an inner not an outer compulsion. It is truth in speech. The one who speaks according to the *rta* is *rtavaka*. Heaven and earth are *rtavan*, true to the rta. It is being which acts with that order and truth on which the cosmos rests, a coming together of cosmic and moral law. A flexible order, unrigid, not a point but a horizon.

But this order is precarious. The opposing word is *anrta*, the forces of darkness and enclosure and untruth, that cleave apart, slowly, the cosmos and the divine and the human.

Forest

In the Madre de Dios, at the heart of the Peruvian Amazon, night is an unbroken susurration. There are hums that are continuous but which come forth and recede, there are hisses that pulsate, sounds that behave like breath. Life stirs in the canopy of the highest trees, on the branches, the forest floor, in the waters of the Las Piedras river that moves through the forest. Above, there is a blinding moon. Below, a mist spreads to cover trees and hang from branches. There is no past or future in this forest, only what is present and breathing and vigilant. Beauty is only a first experience here. Once that beauty is entered there remains only a pre-human, centripetal force. The moon lights up a clearing that has a thatch-roofed house raised on stilts, silent at night. But there behind the sussurations, a puma moves towards the colpa, howler monkeys sleep in the trees, armadillos rest on the forest floor.

Twenty per cent of the Amazon forest is already gone.

The Las Piedras river is brown with silt. Smaller trees and shrubs hang over the water, their branches touching the river's surface. Beyond them taller trees rise in a profusion of species, forming green cliffs on the banks. The sky above is an impenetrable blue. The boat moves slowly over the brown water through the green cliffs on either side, moving with the river as it makes its astonishing bends and turns and moves straight ahead as the river opens out again. Inside the water are catfish, caymans, piranhas, stingrays. A dense murmuring comes from insects and the living of snakes and mammals on the land, broken sometimes by a birdcall. The forest, even in the day, is alert. Around a bend where the river has widened, a tapir walks near a small waterfall. Tapirs are the most primitive mammals on earth and they have lived here for 20 million years. It walks slowly along the white clay banks, a pensive animal, moving through the beginning of the universe.

Since 1990 the Peruvian Amazon has lost 27,73,810 acres of primary rainforest.

The pre-human is magnificent and tenacious, but fragile.

Walking through the forest at noon, sometimes cutting giant leaves to clear a way, stepping over a fallen log, over a stream, inventing paths. Looking closely at the leaves of the quinine tree and biting the bitterness, the menthol plant with its strong smell, the cania from which aspirin is made, the pungent wild garlic which heals fungal infections. The man takes a large bamboo branch in his hands and moves it up and down. It makes a sound like wind moving through great trees. The sound accompanies the Ayahusca ceremony, he says, it accompanies the shaman's song which begins the ritual. The brew is used to heal mental illness, depression and also many of the sorrows that human beings naturally suffer. 'In therapy no one really listens, or can listen. There has to be a deeper change. You have to be pushed to it. Ayahusca is never used for anything but healing, never. Never for enjoyment. You must take it a few times, over months. When you take it, your individuality goes. We don't believe in individuality here. When you take the Ayahusca your individuality goes, you become one with others, you see the beauty on the other side of your sorrows.' Red and blue macaws screech from the crowns of ironwood trees above. 'Most of the shamans are very old now and less and less people will have the knowledge that they did. They are carrying the dying knowledge of a thousand years.'

On the way back, on the red soil in a small clearing, hundreds of blue butterflies hover over the carcass of a snake.

          SHARMISTHA MOHANTY

Forest

The wooden tiger stands in silence. A coir palm tree nearby has small fruit hanging from its flexible branches. Almost as tall as the tree is an iron horse underneath but neither is more than ten inches high. Wood and clay birds sit below among flowers of white sholapith. A long cloth snake curves through all of this as if it were a winding river. This forest is still, it has not been seeded, it will not grow. Its floor is woven from reeds. When the wind suddenly blows nothing in this forest will move. Not far from the tree are the lovers carved in copper who do not look around but only at each other. A bronze turtle sits at the feet of a thin bronze ascetic who is holding his begging bowl and a staff. The colours here come from the materials, light wood, dark iron, earth red clay. The sun lights the tree's branches, falls in a circle on the horse's iron back, makes golden the white flowers and the tiger's tail. The makers of each thing here brought their hands and the *rta* close to one another. The watcher has arranged each thing so that the whole becomes a forest. He has arranged the *rta*.

Plants

While describing the creation of the universe, the Manusmriti says that plants 'possess inner consciousness and have the realisation of both pain and joy.' In the Mahabharata the sage Bhrigu teaches Bharadvaja about the life of plants saying that plants respond to touch, sound, taste and smell in the same way that humans respond with their senses. They have great sensitivity to touch, heat and thunder. They can, in their own way, see, hear, smell, taste, share joy and sorrow, and repair and rejuvenate their damaged parts.

Ritual

Not holding in a wish, a hope, a belief, but exposing it to the light, committing the body. Moulding it, casting it, drawing it, singing it, stitching it, weaving it, lighting it, firing it, dancing it, walking it, climbing it, circling it, chanting it, calling it. Body, mind and heart moving together in perfect intimacy, while looking into what cannot be foreseen, into things whose fate is always uncertain, a harvest, a birth, a death.

The word *ritual* comes from the Latin *ritualis*—that which pertains to *rite* or the Latin *ritus,* cognate with the Sanskrit *riti,* and so related, finally, to the *rta.*

Alpona

My mother makes an alpona on the floor of our home with luminous white rice paste. She paints the ceiling of the Ajanta Caves, somewhere she has never been. The same large concentric circles fill the room, within it bands of flowers and leaves. The centre is always a large flower, a many-petalled lotus. In her right hand she holds a sheer white cloth dipped in the rice paste, she squeezes the rag so the paste flows down her right ring finger that acts as a brush. Within the bands she paints creepers that coil in precisely the same way as in Ajanta, curving up in a crest then down in a trough, and the space in the troughs filled again with a flower or a leaf. There are always stalks of paddy, curving fish, flowers and plants, all meaning abundance. The rhythm is the same, from the second century BCE, the harmony, the balance, the proportion, the way.

The alpona is always drawn from the centre outwards as if from long before Ajanta when they believed that the universe expanded from a point, like a navel. How far did the universe go? *What are the rules? What are the goals? What are the limits?* the Rig Veda asks. This way of drawing a wish, seeking a blessing, is older than we will ever know, perhaps from a time even before these questions were consciously spoken.

It is not what my mother paints. It is the unaware way of drawing out the infinite through profusion, how things are repeated, elaborated, from the navel out, to reflect the variations and intensities of wishing and worship, her way of kneeling forward, of sitting in virasana as she looks down at the circles, how she decides where to end the concentric circles on the outside because the limits are not laid down, her knowledge of creating sacred spaces and then wiping them clean when their use is over, her knowing

that she will make an alpona countless times in the future, how she rides
the crests of her life and her understanding of the troughs, her love for
unstitched cloth.

Alpona

In the villages of Bengal alpona has always risen from agriculture. A domestic ritual, only women were its painters. On specific days of worship they painted their wishes and prayers—rain, a good crop of paddy, fish in the rivers, fertile soil, brimming ponds. Whatever was wished for could be painted—birds, trees, stars, planets.

The paintings were mainly on floors and walls, but also on earthen pots, winnowing trays, low, flat wooden stools on which a bride and her groom would sit, and paddy bins.

Now that the village women must earn by daily labour outside the home, or cut supari for export, the art of the alpona is slowly disappearing. Painting wishes and prayers and manifesting them outside oneself comes from a thousand years of expansive time, the time of the natural world.

Invariable

There are constellations of stains on clothes and sinks and floors and
dishes, galaxies of dirt, dust and cobwebs in corners and hanging from
ceilings, cooking pots with a new kind of debris every hour, burnt milk
to be scrubbed out of whatever it clings to for life, these constellations
appear each day, eternal like the universe, but without its infinite space
that allows the sight to go far and return again with new meanings, the
body is on its hands and knees, the neck hanging down, then standing up
again, leaning out, stretching an arm too far to reach something on a shelf,
straining up and up to get at something else, then bending down, down,
down again, losing balance as it reaches to follow that clump of hair and
dirt that is being blown away, sweat running down the neck and back and
collecting in the armpits as heat surges from the stove, the iron, the oven,
the chulha, the coals, the hot chapattis swelling as the sun burns outside,
either there is standing in the same place or there are imperceptible
movements, in inches, as the body sweeps floors or hangs forward to put
clothes out in the sunlight, for the eyes there is only the very near, a tear on
a blouse, a torn armhole, the threading of needles, sorting methi leaves,
the sky appears at the windows but the eyes have lost the ability to look at
anything without limits, at night an astonishing star hangs above, lighting
up the most acute regrets, but shines no light on how to blunt their
serrated edges, from the shoulder to the wrist and hand the movement
never stops, kneading dough, chopping vegetables, scaling fish, taking the
fat off the meat, lifting the iron, scrubbing the sink, rubbing the healing
gel on someone else's back, the unending arrangement of so much that
is needed, food and clothing and cleanliness, starting over every day, so
that sometimes there is the attempt to look at all of this like the Buddhist
monks who have said the utterly ordinary can also be a path, but this
lasts only a few hours in the utter complexity of life where the simple is in

fact a galaxy away, the simple that is crucial to a contemplative ordinary,
tomorrow the dirt from the potatoes must be scrubbed, the rice cleaned,
the chutneys ground, tasks that remains alive and breathing always, while
the pelvic pain, the flowing of blood comes every month without fail,
making the forward bend a slow painful movement, adding also to the
constellations of stains, when the seasons change there is the novelty of
a ripened heat and sweat that will produce rashes on the skin and fungal
infections although it will be good for the mango pickles left to ferment in
the sun, the rains will bring relief but new places indoors will have to be
found for clothes to dry and not retain a damp smell, insects will attack the
grains, so that the rice will have to be picked through and cleaned, garlic
will blacken if not used up, metal will rust leaving things to be repaired,
there will be no time to watch the rain falling and through it one's own
life, only in winter there may be a brief reprieve from guarding against
the elements, patience and endurance are mined continually from the
deepest depths, if there is any spaciousness it is inside those depths, in
the darkness, and when the sun rises each day it rises on the landscapes
of invariable dailyness, although wide rivers still flow to the sea and the
ocean carries ships to its ports, and roads move through thick forests
and cities, and space stations circle the earth, the number of lives to be
mourned, the numbers lost to dailyness are as infinite as the grains of sand
on the three edges of the oceans that surround the subcontinent.

Guru

Only one painted portrait exists of the family guru. He is seated on the floor with his hands on his lap. A dark brown cloth is wrapped around his body, leaving the right shoulder bare, reaching till the upper part of the thighs. His hair is piled in a knot on top of his head. His eyes have moved that imperceptible distance towards each other, and the painter, though not a master, has achieved the inward look, a centripetal force.

They say the guru was born around 1730. That he dedicated himself to the path of knowledge as a child. That he travelled to the Himalayas and later to Afghanistan and Persia, on foot. That he did not believe in performing miracles. That later he returned to a village in Bengal and built a hut there of bamboo, hay and mud with his own hands. He wanted to show people that there was beauty and dignity in labour. That it was here that his first disciples gathered, Hindu and Muslim. That he told everyone to act with awareness.

More than a hundred years later, a disciple built another hut in which he placed a painting of the guru, a copy of the original. He had been saved by calling on the guru, he said. The hut was outside a big city and sometimes people came to pray there. The little girl brought here many times by her parents and grandparents would remember it for the rest of her life. It was hot and humid inside the hut. Oil lamps shone in the darkness. The painting was large, almost life-sized. Its colours were browns, greys and whites. Palm and mango trees surrounded the hut and the land outside it. It was the only place they had come to worship not a god, but a human being.

Later, they broke down the hut and moved the painting to a large white marble structure. Along with the painting in the centre they added a white marble sculpture, a likeness of the painting. As in a temple, the centre was surrounded by a wide plinth where people could sit and say their prayers to the guru.

According to his early disciples the guru told them that when he was in meditation in the Himalayas, heaps of snow would cover his body and slowly melt away. He told them about being undefined, unbound, but never unsteady.

Soil

Alluvial soil, fecund, where both matter and fate decompose, ashes of ancestors gone, the sweet brown sap of the date palm so loved by everyone, banana leaves, bits of conch shell, warp and weft of torn saris, pieces of sail, husks of paddy, the bronze of bowls, fish bones and scales, the gleam of a grandmother's love, each thing taking its own time to decay. The grandmother, holder of births and nourishment and marriages, of the crucial ordinary, holding the deaths and all her griefs close in absolute silence, the long syllables of her language, the standing at the threshold when someone left, the waiting on the balcony for their return, the sitting on the chair placed exactly in line with the large windows so she could gaze at the sky for a moment, in the soil those windows, the bricks and walls of the large house, living forms swarm around inert grains of matter, mitochondria, bacteria and insects live on things broken and thrown away, our memories deep inside soil, in dark and moist terrain necessary for life, along with hundreds of thousands of worms, ants, bacteria, fungi, most of them still undiscovered by science, gods in the deep riverbeds, melting away rapidly with their bamboo and clay, broken boats of wood, taking longer, pieces of iron lasting the longest, rusting slowly and disintegrating over a hundred years, and we standing on a soil always decomposing and renewing, layer upon layer, on a past that fluctuates but is also stable and continuous.

Transience

In the flowers and mango leaves and oil flames for worship, in the sholapith that the bride and groom must wear at weddings, in the fire that stands witness, the banana tree which is Lakshmi, in the gods sent into rivers to float far away, the fragile, the easily shattered, is always close, and each of these according to the season, the seasons themselves fragile, returning with a variance each time, the body finally becoming fire and ashes, the waters that purify, and people living by the sung and chanted and heard and drawn so much more than the written word, the time of the written and the uttered expanding each other, so that here on the subcontinent there are more times to live by, which brings a kind of undefinable assurance, and on the edge of the radish and spinach fields in the northern plains there is a mud and thatch house made for storing cow dung on which its maker has etched plants and birds and leaves.

Durga

The rains have ended and the autumn skies are a clear blue, without a
cloud. Through these clear skies comes Durga, returning, as legend says,
from her husband's home in the high, cold mountains to be with her
parents again in the forested plains. She is welcomed with joy as the
daughter coming home. Folklore makes tender and tactile what is too
far to touch or love. Durga is light-skinned and beautiful, with dark eyes.
Sarvamangala mangalye. The prayers are in Sanskrit and at the end of it
Durga receives a rain of flowers. The core of the worship though is not to
her image. Its centre is an earthen pot of water, the waters of creation, the
divine womb. The pot is set on a clod of earth on which barley seeds have
been planted. On the top of the pot is a cluster of nine kinds of leaves,
vegetal icons of the goddess, the *navapatrika.*

In the forests and groves of Bengal, near its rivers and ponds, the goddess
was seen as earth, and the plants that the earth seeded. The Durga Puja
is a harvest festival, celebrating the *rta*, the cyclical order of the natural
world. Brahmanism came late to Bengal, not before the third century AD.
Durga was in the trees and plants necessary for everyday life, she was in the
ashoka, the bel, in roots like haldi and of course in the auspicious banana
tree with its many uses. *Shive sarbarthasadhike .* Sanskrit gave only a new,
resonant utterance to that which had been uttered for thousands of years
in other languages. The feminine divine that was the earth and everything
that grew upon it is much older than the invention of history. Durga was
very likely not light-skinned, but dark, like her worshippers, she had no
need for a husband and came alone, and the buffalo demon that she killed
may have been the buffalo that entered the paddy fields and destroyed the
tender rice saplings each season. *Sharanye tryambake Gauri.* Some believe
that the demon was also the demon of drought.

Long before Durga was described in the Devi Mahatmya as the divine
force that fights evil and restores order in the cosmos, as the transcendent
divine principle, she was already in the earth and the waters, in the new
rice saplings, in deep forest groves and shrubs and trees, in the spices
needed every day, in the paddy turned golden at the harvest under clear
skies. *Narayani namastute*. Because the subcontinent does not live only
by sequential time, Durga comes from near and far, from faith and fields,
from history and the primordial, from myth and memory, she is wild
and domestic, complex and simple, in the language of everyday and the
mnemonic rise and fall of Sanskrit.

Sarvamangala mangalye
Shive Sarbarthasadhike
Sharayne tryambake Gauri
Narayani namastute

At the very beginning she may have been without human form, and in
Bengal, a land of primeval forests, she was often worshipped at the foot of a
tree or at a miniature forest made of *sheora* twigs.

Past

The grandparents sit on wicker chairs in the sunlit balcony. Her white sari and his white dhoti are both crumpled, dishevelled, in black and white. She has her aanchal over her head. From the present they seem defenceless, claimed by tradition, without choices, without the knowledge of so much that has changed and been discovered since they were gone. They seem indifferent to being photographed, perhaps they were asked to interrupt what they were doing and sit hastily on the chairs. The way they sit on the chairs is the same way they would have sat on the floor, or the bed, as if the chair did not necessarily hold them with greater firmness.

For a long time, the looking back at the grandparents, born in the early 1900s, was through a patina of time and compassion. What they lacked was very large—the future. But through that inexplicable arc of change that makes things turn, those left behind became the ones who had instead left something behind for those that came after.

They came from the alluvial land on the edge of the Bay of Bengal. Wide rivers at their mouth here and creeks and ponds made the land shine. On a small boat moving through a creek, the branches of trees arched above to form canopies of green. In some seasons if a person stood on the boat and reached towards the branches, ripe fruit gave itself into the hands. The land seeded abundant crop, fish in the rivers and ponds, unending. In the monsoons the rain fell without a break. Then in one malevolent sweep cyclones and floods swept away homes, rivers burst their banks, death and life were held in precarious balance. Over generations the ancestors had seen the land's brutal surprises and its later atonement as the soil seeded the most luminous paddy fields.

The grandparents bore all their griefs in absolute silence but not their love. The crests and troughs of their lives could not be clearly distinguished. Their poise came from a deep alternation of action and inaction, an inheritance of centuries, expressed only through certain lives like theirs, where instinct and discernment had become one.

Ancient

The little girl is lost, to others. She knows where she is, protected by the mountains behind her and the sea ahead, the natural barriers of the subcontinent. She lives on the plains in between, in the forests and by the rivers. Sometimes, when she stands on one leg while playing, she can feel the land moving, in its almost imperceptible tectonic travel northeast. She knows she is not alone. A wind from another geologic age moves through the forests, inconsolable, it creates waves on the rivers. The little girl is embryonic, like the world not yet created from the vast, dark waters at the beginning of time. She contains lives within her but it is as a little child that she remains most potent, most potential. Her grown self comes to visit her often, holding the child in her lap, feeling her unblemished skin. The child wraps her arms around the neck of her older self. They look at one another. The little girl is already able to withstand. But she can also break, because breaking is an ability. She knows what her older self has forgotten, that there is nothing to fear, that they are both capable of crossing their own finitude. Others have lost the little girl in their centrifugal dispersion. But she, travelling in the opposite direction, can see everything, the sorrow that comes from the impermanence of things, the depths of the ordinary, the forests and rivers that surpass understanding, and the way her solitude alternately lights up and darkens the landscape.

Long Cry

The boatman calls out on the wide river, throwing his Bhatiali song over the water, the sharpener of knives calls on the streets, the singer calls out as she elaborates the raga, the baul calls as he plays his ektara and dances. The call travels, beginning in the throat, and goes past the end of the street, the other shore, the other heart, far past its purpose. It may be a call coming from the need to earn and survive, from navigating a river that saves and destroys, from a need to sing to someone who listens. It rises and falls, it recurs, it returns. The call is neither joy or pain, not assertion or negation, not a question or an answer. It is being calling to itself, becoming more than it can ever know.

Grammar

Only language can describe human states that are rarely attained. Abhaya. There is a kind of infinity in the taking away of fear, a vision of something without impediments. The negative definition is a conscious movement, a travelling away, *akrodh*, or a travelling towards, *advaya*. It is a movement not found in a definition that is positive, that does not require a striving for. Here is grammar sprung from the depths, showing a way towards the possible. *Akshara.* The grammar contains the flawed, the possibility of the unflawed, the movement from one to the other, perhaps over a lifetime. *Aditi.* A denial that begins the shedding of a weight, becoming lighter, defying a certain kind of gravity.

Nothing

Nothing, nothing, nothing, not the unbounded sky. Nothing, not the seven and a half acres of land with its fruit and flowering trees each season on which she lives, not the devotion of the Buddhist monks from Cambodia and Thailand who come for the day to visit the great caves and prostrate themselves on their undulating stone floor, not the sudden, unseasonal March thunderstorms and rain and hailstones that last a week and destroy the wheat and leave the farmers bereft, nothing. Nothing, nothing, nothing, not the great Buddha in the caves next door for what can stone do or say or impart or move, nothing. Not her own face hammered and chiselled by her loss as if into its original form. No longer the flabbiness that comes from having received too much love, the stout body shaped and nimble now from the comfort and security of that love suddenly taken away. The passage to beauty not slow but sharp and cleaving, to others, something, to her, nothing, nothing. Not the village women who squat and withstand and tend the land on which these cottages have sat for twenty-one years making a sprawling hotel and retreat for scholars, artists, people of faith, monks and seekers. Not the red-vented bulbuls which come back every twilight to sleep in the tree near the fence, returning when there is barely any light left in the sky so that the bright red on their bodies cannot be separated from the darkness. And almost nothing is what she eats even almost a year after his death, only three spoons of rice and dal at each meal, and perhaps some vegetables, not even rotis which no longer go down her throat, eats this almost nothing as she works at her desk doing accounts and overseeing the whiteness of the towels, the food being cooked in the enormous kitchen, the pruning of the rose bushes. Nothing, nothing, not the nearby small town of ruined medieval mausoleums and graves where Sufis, some of them from Arabia, are buried by the hundreds, now become nothing, the way they wanted. Not the lame hunchback in white who prays at one particular grave each day at sunset and walks slowly backwards till the grave has vanished out of his sight, in time with the light. Not the returning visitor who comes with condolence and compassion, and her tears come without a struggle to stop them as she talks to this visitor and she does not raise a hand to wipe away the wetness, there is no need, I am alone, alone, alone, and nothing, she says. Not the Buddha, nor Shiva nor Durga in the caves across the fence from her land, watching over the centuries, their faces always twice lit, by that imperceptible smile on the face and by fragments of the flexible sunlight that have bent and twisted inside according to the season. Both are sources of light that have never paled even though time has often caused a crack through the head, destroyed a large hand raised in the abhaya mudra, fear not, fear not, leaving the arm as a stump, or smashed a breast, the face has remained lit, a lamp in a windless place, changing nothing, nothing, nothing, nothing, nothing. Nothing, for no hillside exploded and cracked over years, nor its carving by thousands of craftsmen through the centuries, neither the multitude of faiths, neither faith nor its defiance, not the Buddha who worked like a labourer at suffering, his hammer rising and falling in comprehension, nothing can bring to her even a wisp of solace, nothing, nothing, nothing, nothing, nothing. Not the order of the days and seasons that forever return and never falter, and what has been achieved turns into failure, becomes nothing, so that people have to begin all over again, what has already been changes into what is likely to someday become, so that once again the hillside must be exploded, the sky pulled in from above, and till then, perhaps, nothing, nothing, nothing, nothing, nothing.

Birds

The rosy starling appears in flocks on the Indian coral tree as it flowers, in late March and early April. Its body has a rose pink mantle and breast, the head and wings are a deep, shining black. Thirty-one thousand of them die this season, when unseasonal rains come, and with it days and nights of hailstorms. Red-rumped swallows have dark metallic blue and chestnut bodies, and a long, deeply forked tail. They wheel and bank in acrobatic flight as they call their wistful call. Hundreds die in the hailstorms that break and flatten the sugarcane, wheat, oranges, mangoes and pomegranates. Rose-ringed parakeets are bright grass green, with a rose ring around the neck, screech as they fly, raiding fruit orchards and cultivated fields. Fifteen hundred of them die in the hailstorms while they are roosting on teak trees near a farmland. The singing Oriental skylark is a dull brown bird, with a round crest on its head. It rises high and drops low in its flight, sometimes hovering for a time in between. It is among the twenty-six species that are destroyed. Everywhere there are the broken stalks of crops, twigs, leaves and branches. The tiny purple-rumped sunbird is only four inches in size, barely larger than the two-inch hailstones. Purple on the throat and rump, a metallic green crown and shoulder patches, and a deep maroon collar, it is a restless bird of foliage, regularly visiting flowering plants. Sparrows die, and red-vented bulbuls, and mynahs, and the larger francolin partridges, black drongoes, coucals, koels, quails, doves, cattle egrets, blackheaded ibises, painted storks, ruddy shelducks, northern shovellers and owls, bringing the number of deaths to over sixty-five thousand. The land is strewn with the wreckage of broken nests, smashed eggs, and the most delicate bones.

Street

The street rises at one end, suddenly but gently, into a low hill on which a small white church stands. It is closed at one end by this hill, open at the other. The hill protects the street, gives it refuge. The sun rises behind the spire, it sets beyond the open end, at the sea close by but not visible from here. The sea sends in its consequences, a steady afternoon breeze, a knowledge of something endless nearby. Hill and sea and a profusion of trees and flowers are what form this landscape, giving it a very precise disposition and the street bears them all. The street is firm ground, it is vast expanse, conscious of the systole and diastole of the world, it is where the near can open into the far.

Sellers walk by, calling and looking up at the windows, and their calls touch the hill and reflect back, they hover in the air for a longer time, like the calls of birds here, the coucal, sparrow, parrot, golden oriole, magpie, kingfisher, drongo, sunbird, kite, pigeon, crow, koel, mynah, coppersmith barbet and red-vented bulbul, according to their seasons. In the evening hymns flow down from the church, built in 1857, the moon rises from behind the hill, a conch shell is blown somewhere, incense is lit for the gods. Once in a way a brass band accompanies a funeral into the church and out again. An evening wind moves through the leaves of mango, tamarind, jamun, ashoka, gulmohar, coconut, date palm, chikoo and silk cotton trees. The flute seller sometimes comes late, when it is already dark and his notes seem to be suspended in the air for even longer. The street can contain profusion, hold the past without ignoring the future, like the one who is still and watching it knows that the movement of the world is not lineal, it is this now, not before or after.

Among the jasmine, hibiscus, oleander, ashoka and mango flowers, lives rise and fall, those who have spent years looking after things, raising children, recede to their homes in old age and appear on the street with their walking sticks making slow progress step by step, and young people move quickly out onto the street with shoulders angled outward in anticipation. The street is dug up for repairs, perfect paver blocks are torn out and replaced by cement, while new mangoes hang by their stems from branches, chikoos and tamarind grow full, jamun colours the ground purple, dust and grit settle on furniture, masons work on the church wall in the venomous heat, hammers and drills cut through the air, yet the essential silence of the street remains and returns more robust in the evening. With its hill at one end, the street keeps all this from flowing away, holding everything for longer so it can be considered, it offers the ability to slow down the breath and extend the gaze for as long as needed to move to the centre of things, the only element it lets go is the rainwater in the monsoons which it sends down the slope all the way to the sea, and in the enormous bungalow on one side of the chapel, built a century ago in wood with delicately designed balconies, where three generations live, a grandson practises melodies on his trumpet on the open terrace in the evening, as the actress down the street adjusts the pleats of her sari before going on television, and the different species of trees standing on the vacant lot become as thick as a grove making the night deeper, and a life bent forward towards the future like everyone else can slowly straighten up, resisting the feeling that it is incomplete, a life which will see that longing for the extraordinary is a habit, as if the ordinary were not enough.

Forest

The hill at one end of the street is made of basalt, the consequence of a volcanic eruption with its lava flow almost 65 million years ago. The lava gradually hardened into rock, before this southern mass of land joined the northern to form a subcontinent. Much, much later the soil formed from this lava flow, rich in essential minerals, gave rise to trees and plants and forests here, profuse and diverse.

Beyond an old stone wall built from pieces of grey basalt is a plot of empty land on which trees rise. At night it is thick with trees of different heights, the tamarind, the banyan, the palm, the jamun. Nameless vines wind around the trunks and wildflowers sprout from their tendrils. Slim snakes move among the weeds. Night flowers open. To anyone who looks and is impelled, this is a forest, much broader and deeper than it seems, in which to walk away from the world and its forward movement, to answer the need for distances, a *Brihadaranyaka,* a forest where kings have been exiled, where lives have been tested, a *tapovana* because *tapas* needs a forest, where what is tamed can return to wildness, where intention can lose its way, where the skies can clear and the constellations shine. Anyone walking long and far enough may come upon a place where contradictions can be reconciled. There may be a river flowing. All that has narrowed can widen again, the contracted world begin to open. Deep inside the forest there is no need for economy and precision. The superfluous is everywhere. There may be a pond with lotuses. Anyone who watches and enters the forest must do so all alone. When they return it is with all the world.

Street

At dawn a dark brown horse stands despondent near one of the streetlights, waiting. His keeper sleeps against the old stone wall on this quiet street closed at one end where no one will ask him to move away, and where the morning breeze from the sea stays a little longer. The street is transparent. The movement and breadth of everything it bears—the geological and the vegetal, the animal and the human—can be clearly seen. This abundance of time spans makes the street detached, sometimes unprofane.

Funeral

A few times a year, in the late morning or afternoon, the funeral brass band comes down the street. They accompany the coffin and the bereaved, who all walk slowly till the entrance of the small church at the street's end. The first notes can be heard before the small group of people turn he corner and into the street. Then gradually the band can be seen, often leading the procession. They play the trumpet, the French horn, the saxophone, the clarinet, the trombone. They are dressed in worn black suits and ties. The walk from the corner of the street to the church is slow paced, allowing everyone to feel the music, its rise and fall. They play *Amazing Grace*, or *Showers of Blessing*, or *When the Saints Go Marching In*. Sometimes a mourner sings along softly. For the homes on the street where they are from different religions, it is death passing by in music, something they don't have in their own rituals.

The origins of the funeral bands, like many other things in the subcontinent, have vanished under layers of invasions, mergings, sudden turns. The brass band in India most probably emerged from British military bands. Over time they began to play at Indian weddings in the north and at important government events. And in the western part of the country, among the Catholic people, at their funerals.

The leader of the band is a trumpet player who has played at thousands of funerals. Once, he gets a note from a young man who books his band a month in advance. A month later the young man kills himself. He leaves a note saying he wants this brass band at his funeral.

Funeral bands have gradually become more infrequent, playing only at the funerals of the less privileged, those from the Catholic villages inside the bylanes of Bombay. The more sophisticated and urbane choose more solemn, quiet funerals.

The leader says, that sometimes as his band is walking down the street in a funeral procession, someone comes up and says, 'When I die, play for me.'

Trees

One afternoon the tree cutters arrive, their skin the dark brown colour of the bark they will attack. They have been hired to saw off thick branches that are in danger of falling in the heavy rains of the monsoons soon to come. In the May afternoon five men work for hours. The two most agile among them are the ones that climb up, balancing themselves on a branch near the one that they will cut. Then they bring down the axe, attacking the branch till it opens up its light, white, luminous insides. Heavy branches fall to the ground. The men are covered in sawdust, it speckles their faces, their hair and clothes as they work. They speak among themselves in a language not spoken in these parts, their homes far away. Two of them work in a rage that fills their eyes, twists the muscles of their faces and brings a fury of energy to their work. The other three men resent the work as much but express it in the languor and resistance of their movements. At the end they must throw the sawed branches onto a truck and take them away. The logs are heavy and all the men are needed to lift just one onto the back of the truck. Sometimes they look up at the windows on the street through which no one at all watches them work. What they see is closed curtains, blinds all the way down to keep out the heat and the sun. It is almost sunset when they leave, lying on the logs on the back of the truck and looking up at the fading sky.

Everything

They have seen everything. Deserts, salt flats, the Himalayas, the deepest
seas, the thickest forests. The snow leopard moves in the mountains here
and the rhinoceros on the plains. Falcons and peacocks, endless flowers
and fruits and crops. It is a large land, the subcontinent. It has six thousand
varieties of rice, fifteen hundred kinds of mangoes. They have seen the
oldest temples and mausoleums, gods carved on the hillside, palaces
floating on water. Three thousand years of human history makes their
eyes flit here and there, seeking something that this history doesn't offer.
They are tired, without the energy to sift through so much inheritance. It is
cunning that makes them feel alive, renews their depleted energies, brings
robustness to their manipulations. Basavanna and Kabir and Tukaram
surprise them with their irrelevance. In the land of the Buddha an ancient
civilisation eternally perfects its astute insidiousness. They compete and
cheat for the shabbiest shreds of power. The only time when they are
nimble is when they tell everyone else what to do before escaping through
a crack. Otherwise they carry the weight of the stone in temples and caves
and gods, the unbearable heaviness of insights on life and death, and they
can barely move. Having seen and known everything, they understand
that even the greatest striving will bring nothing, that even the highest
goal is utterly treacherous, so that when reached it will strip a person
of the most crucial things, that the only thing to do is to be born and to
die, and to keep praying for luck, that throw of the dice, which is the one
thing that makes everything right, to wait slyly on the sofa till it comes,
in the only land where both tigers and lions move in the forests because
everywhere else it is one or the other, talking ceaselessly of one's small,
dust covered, worn out victories, never listening in silence to anyone else,
they carefully avoid anything expansive in others, living in the land of an
illiterate emperor who sought to understand every different faith, living

in the land of the Buddha and the two birds on the tree, in the land of the
advaita are the greatest separations, because things so often engender
their perfect opposite, and since the gods are ten-armed and the three
strides of a god can cover the three worlds, the final consequence is an
insidious and complete inertia.

City

The woman sitting closer to the pujari says, 'Only this, only this. Otherwise everything is alright, everything.' The pujari nods. He is a dark, thickset man in his early forties perhaps, with a quiet patience in him. He takes some ash from the foot of the Mata's image, says a mantra, and blows the ash from his fingers into the air.

Jari Mari Mata is a face carved in silver, set on top of an orange stone platform. There is a long line to make an offering before her. Below the orange stone, next to the pujari, the two women sit cross-legged on the floor. They are very neatly dressed in nylon saris of bright colours. On the blouses, where the shoulder joins the arm, and near the armpit, there are tiny tears in the fabric which have been carefully darned. They are full breasted, robust women, their hair oiled and tied back.

'Twenty years my husband has had this job, twenty years, and then suddenly to be dismissed...' the woman says. The pujari turns to the Mata's face and says a few more mantras. He touches the orange stone three times. In all his actions he seems patient and kind. He takes a marigold from the heap of coloured flowers before the Mata and places it in her palm. She closes her fingers over it.

The pujari performs the last gestures. He takes the woman's offering of a coconut, raises his sickle and halves the coconut in one stroke. The water inside falls into an enormous brass bowl at his feet. He hands her one half, the other he puts before the face of the Mata. He puts sindur on the women's foreheads and blesses them with his right hand on their heads. The line moves forward just a little in anticipation.

'It's just this,' she says again. 'Just this one thing. We are absolutely fine otherwise.' The other woman nods in agreement. They are reluctant to get up and leave. But the line behind them is beginning to get restless. The women kneel, touch their heads to the orange stone, look for a few moments at the face of Jari Mari Mata and stand up to go.

River

The rocks, the swollen waves of the river, the oars of the boat, the plants, are all tilted towards. Only the sky, far away, retains its horizontal plane. Rama, Sita and Laksman cross the Ganga on their way to exile. The boat is fragile, the river turbulent, untamed. Even a god is a small figure here, identifiable only by his blue body, overwhelmed by the river's swell and fall.

If divided vertically into two equal halves, any life that is not water is on the right. The left, the direction in which the boat is moving, contains nothing but water, distant rocks and an even more distant gleam of sky. The very centre is wave just before it rises. In the foreground the plants are utterly frail.

The bows and arrows that Rama and Lakshman hold are powerless, they cannot pierce the waves. Even a god cannot calm the river or make its waters shallow, even a god must submit sometimes to the natural world, must not control, must allow.

The painter is one of the descendants of the master Nainsukh. Around 1780, when the painter made this, a master himself, had he heard a version of the Ramayana that described the river and the crossing in this way?

In most miniature paintings of the Ramayana, human action forms the centre and the subject. In other paintings, always on land, was the land too firm for the painter to create what he himself may have felt about transformations? Here, in painting Rama crossing over from one life to another, did the painter consider more acutely how everyone must live what cannot be predicted? Did water enable his vision? Did he know that if the swollen river formed the centre of the painting, each viewer would be able to reach through it, and look, at the dangerous crossings of his own life? Was this the only painting where the life of Nainsukh's descendant enters the life of the painting?

This Ganga is grey, the colour of *karuna rasa.*

The green plants in the foreground increase the feeling of *karuna*, deep sadness, lament. There is a homelessness in the rocks that edge the river, a leaving of all that is secure and safe. Movement is the centre of this painting, its end unknown. But *karuna* in Sanskrit is not only lament and sorrow, it is also compassion, and it emerges here from the painter's hands.

It is a compassion reversed, for a god who was present in the painter's world, and to whom he may have prayed in his own life.

Again

Vines and creepers are carved all along temple walls and the lotus blooms on pillar after pillar in the caves, they repeat themselves on the borders of saris woven from cotton and silk, they are painted on the black ceilings of Ajanta, repeated the stories of kings exiled, the forests of their grief, of wars where both sides lose, tales told over and over, songs, images, Durga thrusting the spear into the demon, the Buddha like a full cloud that does not rain, like a lake without ripples, like an unshaken flame, again and again, so that it will never be forgotten, each image, tale and song with the stamina to repeat and recur, not an arrow released once and for all, because nothing in this universe happens only once and never again, things repeat themselves so they can slowly begin to transform, or live their innumerable aspects, the end is not knowledge, the mind's uncountable nuances, but something else, so an image, a tale repeated, a sound, a chant, an utterance, not the word and its meaning but the vowel or the consonant empty of meaning, all with the power to evoke what is crucial, not thought, not wisdom, with the power to invoke, not dream, not imagination, but a brimming and quiescent energy that is always, things repeating, echoing because the universe is imperfect, impermanent, incomplete and always will be, Draupadi's sari will unravel through the centuries, and so to utter, to act, to make the gesture, again and again, till the walk changes and the tilt of the head and the look below the eyelids and the rhythm of the breath, what cannot be willed, only the slow becoming of everything.

Narrow

The air falters and the measure of making, of doing, is undone. To make
is to always work against the unmade, looking far, seeing what is not yet.
Behind what is there are dying herbs and seeds, languages lying in the
undergrowth, beliefs in the deep riverbeds, ways of knowing decomposing
in the soil. The world grows narrower, thinner. Forests are felled and
brushed back from the highways, no dirt or mud anywhere. The two lines
of the road will meet, exactly as the law of perspective says, at infinity.

SHARMISTHA MOHANTY

Mourning

The smell of a father from his shirt, of a mother from her sari, the two so different, still remembered.

Mourn for three days, then the thirteen, then forty, then three hundred and sixty-five. The five elements are close at this time—fire, water, earth, air, space—even when the rituals are done. Fire as grief, water as the days that will flow over and around everything, air as the memories blowing through the house, earth as the heaviness of the body and the feet, space as the emptiness of rooms and beds and the sky.

The time taken to mourn is incalculable, lasting a lifetime. It may be an extreme longing for what will never return. It may turn, from a longing to a sudden velocity, coming suddenly. It may widen, to include the end of the Durga Puja with a Devi moving through the night towards dark water. There is nothing that closes and ends in the course of mourning.

At home the bell metal plates gleamed like gold. A small circle was etched in double lines at the centre. Sometimes stalks of paddy edged the circles. There were small bowls with scalloped edges, all of which shone and reflected back the shadow of a hand. The cooked vegetables and fish took on the metal's shine when served on these large plates, the thin gravies held by their fluted edges. In a little anteroom outside the kitchen these plates and bowls were scrubbed with ash. There is no memory of when they were given away, sold as scrap or handed down to servants. China and glass appeared on the table, lighter, easier to handle, the ash became unnecessary. The table became silent without the resonance of bell metal accidentally being struck, one against the other.

Afternoon

In the afternoon, the day broke into two. The wooden shutters on the windows were closed to keep out the sun, the bedroom turned dark with that hot afternoon darkness, in which the mirror gleamed and sometimes the gold bangles on the women's arms. This was the gap in the day, between its two parts of morning and evening. After lunch the women lay together on a large bed, a grandmother, a mother, an aunt perhaps, and the young girl, three generations together. Their saris were the soft, cool saris of afternoon, not the starched ones they would change into in the evening. They spread out their long hair behind them on the pillows and read a magazine or talked about the simplest things as the young girl, the grandchild, listened, not with particular attention. They talked about a story they had read or the rising price of fish. In those days, when electricity could not be relied upon, even in the large cities, the ceiling fan was often still in the searing and humid afternoons. Hand fans made from palm leaves were used to make a little breeze. The round, beige coloured fans had red and green fish shapes painted on them, sometimes stalks of paddy, or a few strokes of colour. The auspicious, the joyous, was added to something where embellishment was not necessary at all for its use. Once an arm tired the fan needed to be shifted to the other hand. Someone fell asleep while moving the fan and it would drop from their hands making a rustling sound. Someone fell asleep with the fan resting on their chests till the heat woke them again. If anyone was sick or had a fever, the women would take turns fanning them. They never spoke of their sorrows, of their men, of the many changes in their own bodies. An aunt may have spoken of the best pieces of fish that she was never able to have because the men and the elders had to be served first.

A man lay his merchandise on a sheet placed on the pavement of a busy street. He was selling miniature palm-leaf fans, exact replicas of the larger ones. They had miniature paddy stalks and fish painted on them. 'I've come all the way from my village, two hours away. My small son and I made these. It took a month,' he says.

As the fans moved in the afternoon darkness the women slowly drifted in and out of sleep. Their longings and griefs, their sudden joys, did not appear in what they said, even to each other on those protected afternoons. These emerged in the way their eyelids fluttered as they said their prayers to the gods each morning and evening, the angle at which they bowed their heads, the way they felt the quality of a sari by rubbing it between their forefingers, what they cooked for the ones they loved more than the others, the way they all resumed a relationship with a mother or a brother after a fight, without ever referring to what had happened so that slowly it was all forgotten. Through each generation their lives changed and became more individual, more filled with different possibilities. In memories, the afternoons return to indicate that as possibilities open up there are others behind us that have already closed.

Stone

Stone dusk, stone attention, stone hands that indicate, granite and laterite, stone love, stone desire, stone backs ending at perfect waists, lotuses, the shade of stone banyans in which stone bulls rest, red sandstone and basalt, stone daggers plunging through stone rage, stone winds on which the gods are borne upwards, their feet resting on empty space, stone pelvis strength, stone tendril tenderness, minars and courtyards, basalt, pavilions and palaces, stone feet at thresholds, stone eyelids below quiet stone brows, stone serenity, stone fissured, pierced and perforated by each epoch, blackened by soot from the flame burning in the innermost stone room of the gods, stone open to humid air and moss and rain, losing its precision but become the carrier of things that rise and fall, stone broken by human hands prepared over lifetimes, achieving an unforeseen skill over matter, minds evolved through the science and calculations of building, knowing each material, the laying of brick and stone, cutting and carving, and the way the sun rises and falls over the seasons, able to form stone potencies, stone justice, the stone dwarf that grows to cross the three worlds with three strides, stone forgiveness, stone holding down the vision that wind and rain would otherwise blow away, almost moral, because words were not matter enough, stone slowly losing its certainty over millennia, now polysemous, sowing life, sowing death, heavy with the everlasting or weightless as it gives other times to the now, depending on the watcher's gaze.

Mourning

Mourn the empty thousand-pillared halls, each pillar differently carved, through which an inconsolable wind blows, mourn the skill of mastering matter and leaving it behind, mourn the lost reach not of making but becoming, mourn the extraordinary forgotten in the heart of the ordinary, the jewel in the rotted fruit thrown away.

Darkness

Among the hills of Barbagia, in the interior of the island of Sardinia, the darkness is hard and consolidated, like the rocks. It has grains, lines, fissures. A moon shines above but the darkness is unbreakable. It resists all light.

In the Madre de Dios forests of the Amazon, darkness is weightless, translucent. Late at night, as the mist rises and starlight descends, there is the most poised, perfected illumination, just enough to see the contours of faces and things in the clearing, but no more. Among the trees at the edges of the clearing where light will remain far above, pumas, ocelots and tapirs move towards the colpa.

Near the Gaumukh glacier in the Himalayas, the darkness is as thin and transparent as the air. The sky is so close here that hands must shade the eyes when looking at the moon. There is nothing to distract the darkness, and the sky shines an undiluted light on the bare rocks and even into the gorge below.

Once, when there is a power breakdown late at night, this street becomes more present than its inhabitants. The trees throw their leaf shadows on the dark asphalt, mango, jamun and palm leaves touching one another on the ground. The spire of the church becomes a long shadow, cuts through the leaves and glows white in the moonlight.

A rhythmic universe, its measure, its metre, can be extinguished by the power of incessant light. A reconciled opposition disappears, the necessary alternation of seeing and not seeing, a fundamental cadence. Things don't rise and fall as they should, wings, hands and eyes that must open and close begin to stutter.

Migratory birds lose their way and die because of so much light, thousands of them, nocturnal pollinators hesitate and stop, sea turtles looking to hatch by moonlight shining off the waves are thrown onto dry land, bats, plants and fish lose the diurnal undulations they have always lived by.

At night, seen from as far as ninety miles away, the glow over certain cities resembles sunrise.

Mourning

The highways move, with the laws of perspective, towards the horizon, to infinity. Not towards an unknown but an unknown-knowable. There are cleared forests on either side, wilderness hacked, cut, tamed and emptied of life. Along this, complacent cars move forward under vast skies. After long days they return home to large houses on careful streets. And the night, the night so soundless.

Continents crowded with trees and fruit and jaguars and birds of paradise, green coasts perfumed with flowers and fragrant wood, bewildered by the end that they meet, the absolute, complete ruin that comes to them over the oceans.

Laughter in restaurants and bars, in endless eating and drinking, in a million bottles of wine, in the ease of travel to other places where people have so much less.

'They have no …' clothes, property, law, hierarchy, systems, books, god. The more classical civilisations, with the finest art, the most gracious rituals, the boldest philosophies, precious books, are reduced to dirty rivers in which buffalos and humans swim together. An unprecedented self assurance floats like air over the world, a pure air, without any particles of doubt or questions.

The long, broad avenues are spotless, far from mud coloured bodies, mud dirt, mud joy, mud limbs cut as punishment for a moment's rest while building a railway line. The boulevards are assured and filled with purpose, flaunting a brazen beauty, the victory of straight lines that cannot be had without brutal destruction.

Lands and ecologies offering unending sustenance and infinite beauty made over millions of years are hacked, plundered, broken and torn over a few centuries. Far away, the great cities of the world are built.

Mourn these worlds trapped in the new, the continuous need for the original, for inventions. Mourn the worlds that have reshaped continents, diverted rivers and rearranged time and space. Mourn the cartographers making maps in their own image, expanding and contracting land masses. Mourn the universal values made from a manipulated universe.

Sugar, coffee, cocoa, silver and gold, cotton, muslin, corn, tomatoes, potatoes, rubies, pearls, bananas, pepper, cinnamon, cardamom, cloves, plucked, mined, looted.

Mourn the eye's equivocal gaze in the lush, warm continents, as they move towards only one possible future, that sees no choice, only ambiguities that can never be resolved. Mourn the permanent uncertainty and bitter doubt it brings in its wake. Mourn the cold, ice filled lands that see suffering as a human aberration. Mourn the waning knowledge everywhere of how to live through suffering, to turn mud into stars.

'Enlightenment ideas and values—critical scrutiny of all assumptions, open debate, scientific research, progress and tolerance—have marked the museum since its foundation', says the British Museum.

In the great museums, some of them built on fortunes made from the brutal sugar plantations worked by slaves, or fortunes made from Empire, others with loot from far away places, the world's past is preserved carefully with gloved hands. Objects glow in the mellow light to be watched, without the gestures and rituals and touch that must accompany them and give them life. There is a Buddha, with the eyes half closed and looking inward, the lightest suggestion of a robe, the body revealing neither muscles or tension, yet utterly awake.

There was no likeness of the Buddha left behind after his death. It took five hundred years for the first images of the Buddha to appear, helped by the growing presence of several anthropomorphic traditions. A few more centuries passed before the image reached perfection. The stone carvers slowly abandoned size and massiveness in the image, determination and purpose, all the elements of earthly power. They understood that the Buddha's power was elsewhere and they acquired the material skills to manifest this. Gradually, the Buddha image achieved the luminous inner glow of wisdom, the quality of *karuna*, the perfect discipline of the body, mind and senses, possessed by one who has attained *bodhi*. It was the end of a quest. The image would remain as a reminder of the perfected being.

Mourn a world where all change is gain, all equilibrium loss, all discernments transient.

Muslin

From the land of rivers wide as seas, from the land where the largest delta on earth receives the Brahmaputra and the Ganga and their tributaries as they flow into the Bay of Bengal, from the land of alluvial abundance and elation, from the land of floods and ruin, a land of sharpest extremes, came the lightest, finest cloth ever seen, the Bengal muslin, through which the lines on a hand could be counted. A Chinese traveller, Yuan Chwang, who came to Bengal in the seventh century, said the cloth was 'like the light vapours of dawn.'

Muslin was spun only from the *phuti karpas* variety of cotton, short stapled and silklike. It grew along the banks of the Meghna river. There were attempts to transplant it to other areas within the subcontinent and abroad, but it never did grow anywhere else. No one knows the precise reason why it was only this particular stretch of land that yielded the most subtle variety of cotton. So many elements came together, the particular fertility of the soil with the presence of silica, the moist heat, the combination of river and sea temperatures, the quality of the water just before it reached the bay, to create this cloth as light and transparent as air.

The Mahabharata says a muslin cloth was given to Yudhisthira at a Rajasuya sacrifice. It was presented at the court of King Harsha and the court poet Banabhatta wrote poems about muslin. It was worn by Mughal emperors and can still be seen in the diaphanous kurtas and angarakhas and *orhnis* in miniature paintings. They called it by many names according to the particular treatment of the cloth—*jamdani, abrawan, shaman, nayansukh.*

During Akbar's reign the *mulmul khas* began to be made exclusively for the emperor and the imperial household. Akbar thought it was the perfect fabric for the Indian summer. He designed the Mughal *jama*, a man's kurta with a fitted top and a pleated skirt falling below the knees.

In the villages near the Meghna women cleaned the cotton and then combed it with the jawbone of a fish, the *boal*, found in abundance in the rivers. This jawbone forms an arc, with very fine teeth on the inner surface, making a perfect comb, allowing the finest impurities to pass through. The cotton was then pressed. The cleaned and pressed cotton was now teased or bowed with a *dhunkara*, a bamboo bow with a string made of silk or the midrib of a banana tree. Women held the bow above a pile of cotton and strummed the string. With each vibration the lighter cotton would separate from the heavier fibres and it was this lighter cotton that was spun into muslin. It was always young women who did the strumming because they had the lightest and most deft fingers that could create the most subtle vibrations.

While spinning the *phuti karpas* light was needed to properly see the finest fibres, and the humid air to keep the cotton pliant. The spinning was done in the very early mornings and in the late afternoons, avoiding the heat of the day.

Trade in muslin grew to its height between the sixteenth and eighteenth centuries. From Bengal it travelled to Arabia, clothed Turkish kings in the Ottoman Empire, went to Central Asia, China, Sumatra, New Guinea and later to London and Hamburg, Lisbon and Copenhagen, to the eastern coast of America. Empress Josephine and Marie Antoinette both had dresses made in muslin.

The work of farming the *phuti karpas* to creating the muslin cloth was a process that took time and intense human labour. Men and women, Hindus and Muslims, castes both higher and lower in the hierarchy worked together and had their specific roles. Often the river goddess Dhaleshwari was invoked in prayers and songs by both Muslims and Hindus before work was begun. The work became even more minute when stylised motifs were woven into the cloth. Passed down over generations they were motifs made from flowers, leaves, fruits, sweets and animals, that the weavers themselves farmed, touched, ate every day.

'It was the British intruder who broke up the Indian hand-loom and destroyed the spinning wheel. England began with driving the Indian cottons from the European market; it then introduced twist into Hindustan, and in the end inundated the very mother country of cotton with cottons…' wrote Marx, in *The British Rule in India, New York Herald Tribune*, 1853.

Bengal muslin would have first clothed those who lived there, with their sturdy and robust bodies. Perhaps first the women with their dark, hydrated skins, covered on especially humid summer days with a layer of sweat. Its lightness and transparency made it an erotic fabric against which the long, black hair and large black eyes would shine. It allowed our body to breathe, for the evening wind over the Meghna to pass through it and cool the skin. For men, it would have been a dhoti as light as air, perhaps with the thinnest border woven at the edges. The humid climate, the monsoons, kept our skin moist, made our hair thick, and looking far over the wide rivers gave us our large eyes.

The Meghna still flows, thirteen kilometres in width at its widest point, its other bank too far to see. Deep green islands sometimes emerge from the water. The river songs sung by boatmen here over the centuries rise high and fall low over the water's expanse. If there is anything this landscape knows, it is the inevitability of alternations. The delta is one of the most fertile lands on earth producing a rare diversity and profusion of crops. But the rivers swell and rise in the monsoons, often overflowing their banks and villages nearby, there are storms and cyclones that bring loss and ruin. The songs know that what disappears may never return.

Hands

Those with the roughest hands have created the softest, finest fabric that clothed emperors and royal courts, the most intricate carvings of stone that have lasted three thousand years, the infinite weaves of bamboo on which to lie and rest, they have achieved this with the most basic tools and techniques that could not be hurried, they have beaten iron, copper and bronze into pillars and bowls brimming with carved flowers and leaves, fired clay into goddesses and horses and terracotta temples, all of this with the most subtle and complex knowledge of the materials they crafted.

The silence of these hands and implements is a prelude to the silence of museums.

Earth

The mat made from water reeds has a simple pattern of long lines, with short lines between them. The eye receives rest from this surface, flowing onward with the long lines and pausing at the short, the mat's rhythm as elemental as breath. As the sun falls on the reed mat it opens up a long gaze through which the slender, green reeds can be seen, standing in the shallow waters of the wetlands they come from. Wild birds make their home in these reeds and fish take shelter in their dense roots. Through the copper jar the ore is reached, all the way into the earth's crust, through the clay pitcher, earth. These objects bring with them their sources, whole forests, ponds and hills. They have been cut, fired or shaped, but they have not been severed from the earth. Made from elemental things they are related to one another. In the pitcher, water and earth meet, in the hand fan, leaf and air, on the mat, the human body and reeds. At twilight the shadows of birds pass over them as they would over the landscape they were made from.

Zebra

The inscription on this painting is in Jehangir's hand. *Hamrah-yi Mir Ja'far avardah budand sanah 1030 wa sabih-I inra Nadir ul-'Asri Ustad Mansure kasidah sanah 16.* (A mule which the Rumis, Turks, in company of Mir Ja'far had brought from the Habs country, Abyssinia, in the year 1621 and Nadir ul-'Asri Ustad Mansur has drawn it in the regnal year 16.)

An Abyssinian zebra, also known as Burchell's Zebra, was presented to Jehangir at the commencement of his sixteenth regnal year, 1621. The zebra was brought by Mir Ja'far, who was the governor of Surat and Cambay, where he also traded as a merchant. Jehangir kept records of all the plants, flowers and animals that he saw and observed keenly, in his book, the *Tuzuk-i-Jehangiri*. On seeing the zebra, he wrote in the *Tuzuk*: 'At this time I saw a wild ass, exceedingly strange in appearance, exactly like a tiger. From the tip of the nose to the tail and from the point of the ear to the top of the hoof, black markings, large or small, suitable to their position were seen on it. Round the eyes there was an exceedingly fine black line. One might say that the painter of fate, with a strange brush, had left it on the page of the world. As it was strange, some people imagined that it had been coloured. After minute enquiry into the truth, it became known that the Lord of the World was its Creator. As it was a rarity, it was included among the gifts sent to my brother Shah Abbas.'

Jehangir is an emperor, he rules through lineage and not by the choice of the people. Ustad Mansur is a court painter, he must paint what he has been asked. And the zebra, helpless, brought as an exhibit for human wonder, passing as a gift from one emperor to another, suffering its strange fate, travelling from Abyssinia to India and then to Persia for Shah Abbas.

Yet there is beauty here, in the compassionate accuracy of the painting, in Ustad Mansur's gifted hands, in Jehangir's capacity for wonder, in the painting left behind for other ages which experience the wonder, not of the zebra, but of the painting and how it came to be made.

Lineage

Bodhidharma, the Buddhist monk who is said to have taken Buddhism to China, had a guru who was a woman. This knowledge has largely been lost, as possibly that of many other women in the Buddhist lineage. But archaeological discoveries in the south of India have confirmed her existence. The oral and historical traditions of Kerala contain details about her life. And the Zen lineage of Korea speaks of her.

She knows where she is, protected by the mountains behind her and the sea ahead, the natural barriers of the subcontinent.

Prajnatara was an orphan who did not even know her own name. She called herself Keyura, which meant bracelet or necklace. Prajnatara was a beggar till she met the great master Punyamitra and became his disciple. He believed she was the manifestation of the Bodhisattva Mahastamaprapta, or Great Strength of Compassion. Keyura renounced the world, taking the name Prajnatara.

She knows she is not alone. A wind from another geological age moves through the forests and groves, inconsolable, it creates waves on the rivers.

When the Hun invasions of the fourth and fifth centuries devastated northern India, destabilising the Gupta Empire, Prajnatara travelled south to the home country of her master Punyamitra. She was invited to teach in Kanchipuram by the reigning king Simhavarman. She began teaching the king's youngest son, who caught her attention because of his unusual nature. After the death of his father, Prajnatara helped him to become a fully ordained monk and gave him the name Bodhidharma. It is said that she asked him to take the teachings to China.

But she, travelling in the opposite direction, can see everything, the sorrow that comes from the impermanence of things, the depths of the ordinary, the forests and rivers that surpass understanding.

Forest

On this peninsula, a forest is always immeasurable, even if it is not vast. It has always held deception and transparence, the rakshas and the ascetic, the exiled king and the ashram. It has been the place of protection and danger, where power felt alone and the tamed returned to wildness. It is nowhere and the very source, it is the freedom to break the certainty of fate, so that someone can be no longer what they once were, the forest not only topographical but a desire, not noun but verb, centripetal force.

Words

Words, less and less read, written, heard, seem to recede far, as a seen reality comes forward. Images that show the husk of the world. The word comes from the infinite space of consciousness and returns into it, with slowness, with afterness. Images of reality glide over the retina with ease. Within words the leopard walks the streets only a few steps behind, so it is crucial to be vigilant. From words begin the unseen, unproven truths. Inside words are born all asking, whether in doubt or prayer. It is not in the blackness of space, searching for planets, that we are most original, it is in our words.

In the evening the little children play together for hours and at the end say goodbye many times. As if they may not have heard each other, as if they were not sure they said it right. Or perhaps to express the many meanings of the word in their hearts. *I don't want to leave you. It was beautiful to be together. We will see each other tomorrow.* Even if they don't yet really know how soon tomorrow will come. Perhaps they love the saying of things, their newly acquired ability to speak.

Truth

When someone left we said, *esho,* come again, and they said, *aaschi,* I will return. A breath path was made between one person and another, or rather the breath path was acknowledged, because it was already there. It was there with a recent acquaintance or with a brother, even with someone who did not evoke tenderness. To say what you did not mean was necessary to keep the breath paths open. When a guest said they were leaving, you asked them to stay a little while longer even if you didn't really want them to stay. What the heart felt and what the ritual asked for were not the same. In that distance there was infinite space, for everyone.

Mourning

There are no rituals to mourn things that have passed—objects, landscapes, words. No fires to be lit or circled, no ashes to be thrown into rivers.

Ordinary

Early in the morning large leaves fallen from the badam tree are swept away by street cleaners with long, stiff brooms. The leaves are dry, yellowish on one side and light red on the other. Ordinary these leaves, the rustling sound of sweeping that assures things are as they should be, ordinary the abundant shade the tree provides on a city street. A young man appears selling hot tea, pouring it from his enormous kettle into tiny paper cups. He sells to the men who guard the high rises all day and night, through the heat and rain. Unexceptional the young man and his customers, the sunrise, the beginning of a new day.

In a village in Peru, ordinary the unforgettable certainty of the blue sky,
the thatch-roofed stone church from centuries ago in the central square,
commonplace the men and women with broad, sturdy faces, who wait
to sell mineral water and fruit to anyone passing through, ordinary their
gaze, calm and with infinite patience.

In the village of Jinze a few hours' drive from Shanghai, a man sits fishing
in a canal. It is a still, late afternoon and the trees on the banks throw their
shadows on the water turning it the colour of dark jade. On the small
bridge that crosses the water an old woman rides by on a bicycle with a
cart attached to it. The cart is filled with discarded cardboard boxes.

Climate and land mark these faces, their faithfulness to the latitudes and longitudes they live in, and sometimes their history, more aleatory than the winds and the land.

On the narrow cobblestoned streets of Mamoida village in Sardinia an old woman steps out of a house in the black dress that all old women seem to wear there. Her face is rugged and striated, like the rocky terrain she lives in. 'Buona notte' the visitor says. 'Buona sera' she answers with a smile, gently correcting the mistake. She stands there and smiles for a moment longer, then turns and walks away. It is indeed evening, more translucent and lighter than night.

Each landscape is commonplace, provincial, and the ordinary is everywhere, covering the continents where there are no cities and sometimes even within them, and when someone mooring a boat on a twilight river turns and looks at a visitor the gaze is empty, as though they had been told that their rivers and trees were nothing, their mountains and hills nothing, planting the rice nothing, passing down a ritual nothing, so their eyes look outward the way nothing looks at everything.

Acknowledgements

Excerpts from *Extinctions* have appeared in *Granta*, Indian Cultural Forum, *Witness: The Red River Book of Poetry of Dissent*, *Pratilipi*, *Almost Island* and *Lexikon der sperrigen Wörter* in Germany. *Mourning* (p. 25), *Ancient* (p. 49) and *Narrow* (p. 69) were created as part of a poetry conversation with British poet David Herd, included in *Poetry and Covid: An Anthology* (Shearsman Press, UK).

All photographs by the author, except in *Smile* (p. 26), *A Dvarpala at the entrance to one of the caves at Elephanta, from the 6th-7th century BC*, photo by kind permission of Bharath Ramamrutham.

Painting of the zebra in *Sunset* (p. 11) and in *Zebra* (p. 87) is Burchell's Zebra, inscribed by Jehangir and drawn by Nadil ul-Asri Ustad Mansur in 1621, Minto Album, Victoria and Albert Museum. By kind permission of the museum.

In *Kajol* (p. 16), the following lines are from Chandogya Upanishad:

The earth, in a certain way, meditates.
The atmosphere, in a certain way, meditates.

Painting in *River* (p. 66) is titled *Rama and Sita Crossing the Ganges in Exile*. By kind permission of Museum Rietberg, Zurich

The photograph of the Bhutas (p. 70) is taken at the collection of the late Vijayanath Shenoy, now called the Hasta Shilpa Heritage Village.

For *Muslin* (p. 81), the book *Muslin*, by Saiful Islam, was used as a reference.